NORMAL
is just a
SETTING
on the
DRYER

NORMAL
is just a
SETTING
on the
DRYER

*And Other Lessons from
the Real Real World*

by Adair Lara
Illustrations by Roxanna Bikadoroff

CHRONICLE BOOKS
SAN FRANCISCO

Text copyright © 2003 by **Adair Lara**
Illustrations copyright © 2003 by **Roxanna Bikadoroff**

"Come From the Heart"
Words and music by Susanna Clark and Richard Leigh
© 1987 EMI April Music Inc., GSC Music and Lion-Hearted Music
All rights controlled and administered by EMI April Music Inc.
All rights reserved. International copyright secured. Used by
permission.

Library of Congress Cataloging-in-Publication Data

Lara, Adair.
    Normal is only a setting on the dryer: and other lessons
    from the real, real world / by Adair Lara; illustrations
    by Roxanna Bikadoroff.
        p.   cm.
    ISBN 0-8118-3824-2
    1. American wit and humor.
I. Title.
PN6165 .L37   2003
814'.6--dc21   2002011100

Manufactured in **Canada**
Designed by **Public**

Distributed in Canada by **Raincoast Books**
9050 Shaughnessy Street
Vancouver, British Columbia V6P 6E5

10 9 8 7 6 5 4

Chronicle Books LLC
85 Second Street
San Francisco, California 94105

www.chroniclebooks.com

Work like you don't need the money.
Love like you've never been hurt.
Dance like nobody's watchin'.

– *"Come From the Heart"*

"In what sense has Maria Shriver ever lived in the real world?"

my husband, Bill, asked me over breakfast one morning. He showed me the full-page magazine ad for Maria Shriver's book, *Ten Things I Wish I'd Known Before I Went Out into the Real World*.

"What?" I said. I was putting ointment on a deep scratch from having tried to toilet train the cat. I had bought a kit for this purpose, a cardboard ring that went over the toilet bowl that the cat used during its potty-training phase.

"This, from a Kennedy cousin who's married to Arnold Schwarzenegger? Where's the real world in that?" Bill continued, rattling the paper at me.

Shriver's book prompted me to ask the people I know who live in the *actual* real world what they wished they'd known. I did ask friends and relatives and neighbors of mine from the actual real world what they have found out by knocking around in it. In this book you'll find their hard-won wisdom from that strangest of all frontiers, ordinary life.

How much stranger can ordinary life get than feline toilet training? Which did not go well; as she fell through the cardboard, she leapt out of the toilet, soaking wet. I grabbed her, and ten terrified claws sank into the tender flesh of my arm.

So, for the things I wish I'd known, I'll go first: When the instructions on the flimsy plastic cat-toilet-trainer say "The cat must weigh no more than twelve pounds," **weigh the cat.**

The only really good advice
that I remember my mother
ever gave me was,

"Go! You might
meet somebody!"

Never buy shoes or a hat
by mail order.

Drink wine, save old love letters,

listen to vintage Van Morrison . . .

However,

do not blast Morrison's music and make short order of a bottle of wine while reading those old love letters, or you'll find yourself thinking now would be the perfect time to make a long-distance phone call to their author.

Waiting a year to start
college so I could help sail
a boat to Europe with seven
other friends would have
been the better choice.

Forget marketing and calculus.
Now that I know better, I'm going back
to school to take the right stuff: astronomy,
geology, Russian, French cooking,
and the art of massage.

Forgive yourself the big mistake.

It isn't the end of your life. It will not define
who you are, unless you stay stuck on it.

If you're not positive
a pair of shoes fits,
they don't.

To dislodge a bad song
that's stuck in your head,
sing the national anthem.

If you see a bird you can't recognize,
just say with quiet authority, *"It's a finch,"*
and it most likely will be.

If you still think your friends are normal, then the friendships probably have room to deepen.

Normal is just a setting on the dryer.

The five essential words for
a healthy relationship are
"I apologize" and "You are right."

Not to explain or complain
is possibly the best advice that could
be given to anyone. At the very least,
do not supply the rocks that will
be thrown at you.

Take Spanish, not German.

My most hated subject was Latin.
I got C's all four years I took the subject.
Yet my affection for words, my ability to discover their
meaning, and my fascination with ancient Rome stem
from those hated studies. I wish now I had taken
the language more seriously.

The grass is never truly greener on the other side, and it always has the same amount of weeds as your side.

Bald men are sexy.

If the dog gets his nose stuck in the toaster, he's earned the bagel.

How much did your most comfy shoes cost? Add ten dollars and buy a bra for that amount.

Wine, heavy cream, and salt can make you look like a genius in the kitchen.

Expensive hotels
are rarely worth it.

Cheap hotels
are hell.

Go for the middle range.

Give the people you love
some slack.

You win a few, you lose a few,
and some get rained out,

but you dress for all the games.

To start a conversation with an older person, ask her about the best dog she ever had.

Simply being on time for work every day can get you a good performance review all by itself.

Liver really *is* good for you.

Never leave a place where you're having a good time to go somewhere else where you only **think** you'll have a better time.

Sing out loud in the car, even—
or especially—if it embarrasses the
others in the car.

When the doorbell rings after you have just
undressed for the shower and you decide to
answer it, make sure that the bike shorts you
throw back on are not inside out.

Don't assume that everyone can be your friend. Five close friends who are in it for the long haul are worth a hundred acquaintances.

Always know how to break into your own house.

When dining out, start with the most
unlikable thing on your plate.

(okra, sparrow tongues, blowfish)

This ensures:

1. you will please
the hostess;

2. everything else
will taste better
by comparison;

3. the dread of eating the
aforementioned will be lifted
and you will enjoy the rest of
the meal unencumbered
by anticipation;

4. you might learn to like
something new.

Any and all compliments can
be handled by simply saying

"Thank you,"

though it helps if you say it
with a Southern accent.

You will never win an argument
with a meter maid.

No books will ever be as good as the
ones you loved as a child.

To anyone keeping a journal, especially a young person, write down: bits of conversation; small domestic crises; the concrete, common things. Looking at mine from forty-five years ago, after reading through various useless examples of introspective angst and philosophical musings, I came across the following useful detail: "It's one o'clock at night, and Mom and Dad are in the front room arguing. Dad's threatening to turn on all the lights in the house and wake everybody. He's shouting,

'How in hell can you deduct anything from nine dollars!'"

When baking, follow the directions.
When cooking, go by your own taste.

Never continue
dating anyone who is
rude to the waiter.

I read this for years on the side
of every box of sparklers on the Fourth
of July, and I'm still glad to know it:
Do Not Touch Glowing Wire.

Never have sex if you
don't want to.

Take the train.

Pull over for the idiots and let them pass, even when you are going fast already.

At hard times I ask myself

"How do I feel?
          "What do I want?"

I also use it whenever
I'm at a loss for words or
thoughts.

No matter how crappy you feel,
wearing black will class you up.

Never pass up an opportunity to pee.

Just because things don't work out the
way you planned them doesn't mean
they didn't work out well.

Even if you plan to have only one child, buy
the $300 carriage that converts to a stroller,
instead of the $175 stroller.

Ignore any restaurant
reviewer who uses the words

slathered   or   *redolent.*

Don't be afraid to use the color orange in the garden.

Marry the kindest person you know.

It's never too late to change careers.

Always double the recipes for risotto and chocolate chip cookies; then share accordingly.

Patronize restaurants where the waitresses call you "hon."

You must be
present to win.

That cheesy commercial about being kind to your siblings because they're your closest link to your past and the only people likely to stay with you in the future?

It's right.

You can't fix every problem
in your children's lives.

I always trust people who have had some
kind of a crack-up in their life.

Whenever people say they hate
to say something, they actually
love to say it.

No matter how conservative and stuffy and rigid and career obsessed you may think you are, it's impossible to move to San Francisco and not soften a bit.

Blame your parents and get on with your life.

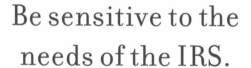

Be sensitive to the
needs of the IRS.

We're all tourists.

If only someone had told me the body I loathed
in my twenties would be the body I wistfully
longed for in my thirties!

Getting angry at the cat for sneaking out and yelling that the stupid thing can stay out all night does not stop you from getting up at four in the morning to see if it's cold and wants in.

Don't buy a car on the same day you see it.
Make yourself wait a day and then take
somebody with you. Above all never buy
a Ford Tempo from a downtown lot on
a rainy Sunday.

Don't go shopping for a couch right after attending a cocktail party where your host served margaritas.

Figure out where you want to live,

and go live there.

Everything else will follow.

Always be in the middle of a book.

Vintage clothing is only for young girls.

If something seems
overly difficult, you are
probably doing it wrong.

Never fry bacon
in the nude.

Vacations are exhausting.

A woman of a certain age should be
wary of hair past her shoulders.

When in doubt,
stir the sauce.

Never lend money you
need to get back.

Waste as much time as possible;

otherwise you end up doing a lot of things
you really don't want to do.

Perms are always a bad idea.

Follow the fat cat.
He must be eating something good.

For hair to be easy it has to
be short or long. Anything
in between is work.

Remodeling takes twice as long and costs
twice as much as you think it will.

If he tells you he has trouble
committing, believe him.

"Hand wash" really means
"Wash on gentle cycle."

Otherwise, believe washing
instructions, especially
"Dry clean only."

Go to

Italy.

Everybody has twenty-five words they misspell. Learn your twenty-five, and presto! You're a good speller.

Be nice to other people.

Compliments from other women
really *do* count.

Never tell anyone you can
type or play the piano.

Don't learn how to start
the lawn mower.

Many women look for a bargain in something they wear a lot—be it a skirt for work or a pair of jeans—and then go off and spend the equivalent of the GNP of a small South American country on a ball gown to be worn only once.

Better to look great every day, in expensive jeans or expensive work suits.

And let's face it, you can't tell whether cocktail dresses are cheap because who drinks cocktails with the lights up?

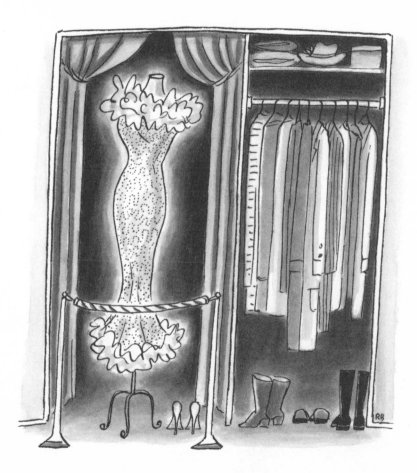

The most important
thing a father can do
for his children is to
love their mother.

Don't wear a white shirt and
drink grape juice while driving
to school.

Never start smoking.

Good judgment comes from experience. And a lot of that comes from bad judgment.

If you find yourself in a hole, the first thing to do is stop digging.

You can raise your children
only as far as the front door.

You will immediately calm
down if you remove your shoes
and socks and walk barefoot.

Things always look better after a long bath with a trashy novel.

When you drink Diet Mountain Dew,
people judge you. Pay no mind.

If someone wants to give you money, take it and say thank you.

Talk straight,

be a little chaste now
and then to increase
your enjoyment of the
blowouts,

and watch for
the humor.

There are many ways to lose battles;
first among them is engaging in battles.

If people understood Shakespeare, they'd leave the theater in their underpants, supporting one another.

Sobriety is the condition for which
alcohol is the specific.

Expectations are premeditated resentments.

Wear cheap pants if you must,
but never cheap shoes.

The best accessory is an attitude.
Wear it as if you mean it.

Your boss is not your friend.

Your mother isn't always right,
but a lot of the time, she is.

Simple gifts from the heart mean
more than expensive ones—

*but that's no reason to refuse
a new stereo.*

No one should talk
more than one-third
of the time.

Pet the kitty.

Don't date any man who is
between the ages of twenty
and twenty-four. No good
can come of it.

If it takes more than three people to make a decision, the worst decision will always be chosen.

A hike can do more than therapy.

Getting started is the hardest part.

The garment has to fit at the
moment of purchase.

Nobody is so good at their job that they can't be fired. Bosses are willing to live with lower productivity to get rid of some-one they see as not fitting in.

The hardest things that will
be asked of you are

1. understand
   yourself,

2.
   understand one
   other person,

and

3. raise a child.

If you said you would bring the birthday cake,
bring the birthday cake.

Return smiles.

Always wear your helmet.

Pick one favorite movie that makes you laugh, another that shakes you up, and a third that makes you cry.

> *Harold and Maude, Psycho,*
> and *E.T.* work for me.

Never give yourself
a haircut after
three martinis.

Comfort men,

because they can't stand as much physical pain
as they'd like you to think. I'm a dental
hygienist, and the men will say, *"Fine, fine,"*
when I ask if it hurts, then go home and tell
their girlfriends I hurt them.

Fancy cars do not impress girls.

Sometimes a woman wants to do nothing
about dinner. A man has no concept of that—
doing nothing about dinner.

Listen to what I mean,
not what I say.

Humor your mother
and father.

Wooden toys aren't as neat as
grown-ups think they are.

Everyday competence—learning to stack the
dishwasher, sew on a button, do the laundry—can be
surprisingly satisfying.

No one knows your children better than you do.
Trust your own judgment. You can go nuts trying
out other people's theories.

Write at least one song or poem, especially if you don't think you can, and read or sing it to the person you love.

You don't have to turn
out like your parents.

The joy of travel is not in finding
so many answers,

but in finding so many questions.

Never eat in a restaurant that has pictures
of the food on the menu.

No one wants that handmade crap.

If you can't get along on a vacation, for
God's sake don't move in together.

Monogamy is fattening,

but worth it.

Don't teach your baby to read until she's two, and certainly never call her "*gifted*." There are long years between Gifted and Eccentric, and most of us fill them with Trouble.

Handicaps are a matter
of perception, *not of fact.*

I wish I had known
I was pretty.

Make a wonderland of your own bog.

It's the only way.

Every misfortune is also an
opportunity, even if it takes
a little time to stop sobbing.

The best answer when turning down a request is to say, "I'm terribly sorry, that's just impossible." Never explain—the other person may be able to override your rationale, or, worse yet, determine you are lying. No matter what she says, or what questions she may ask about your reasons or motives, just repeat,

"I'm terribly sorry, that's just impossible."

If you want the police to come quickly, tell them
you think you saw a gun; if you want to avoid
waiting in the E.R., no matter what you're there
for, tell them you can't breathe.

Always make two appointments when you first call your HMO, as the first one will be a waste of time.

Never get involved with a flamenco dancer, no matter how gorgeous, whether he is from New Jersey or Peru.

Never dive into anything if you
can't see the bottom.

For years my husband argued that we could not have a baby because our condo wasn't big enough. Finally I told him,

"You don't make room for a baby in your home. You make room in your heart."

Wear tights a size larger than
the package recommends,
and you won't get runners.

If you don't want to look like an
American tourist, wander around
for hours with an interested but
confident look and then take a taxi
back to your hotel.

Home is where you were a child and where you return a child.

You should usually qualify almost everything you say.

If a thing goes without saying, let it.

Walking is the best form of transportation, because you arrive at your destination smarter.

The more
you hurry,

the slower you go.

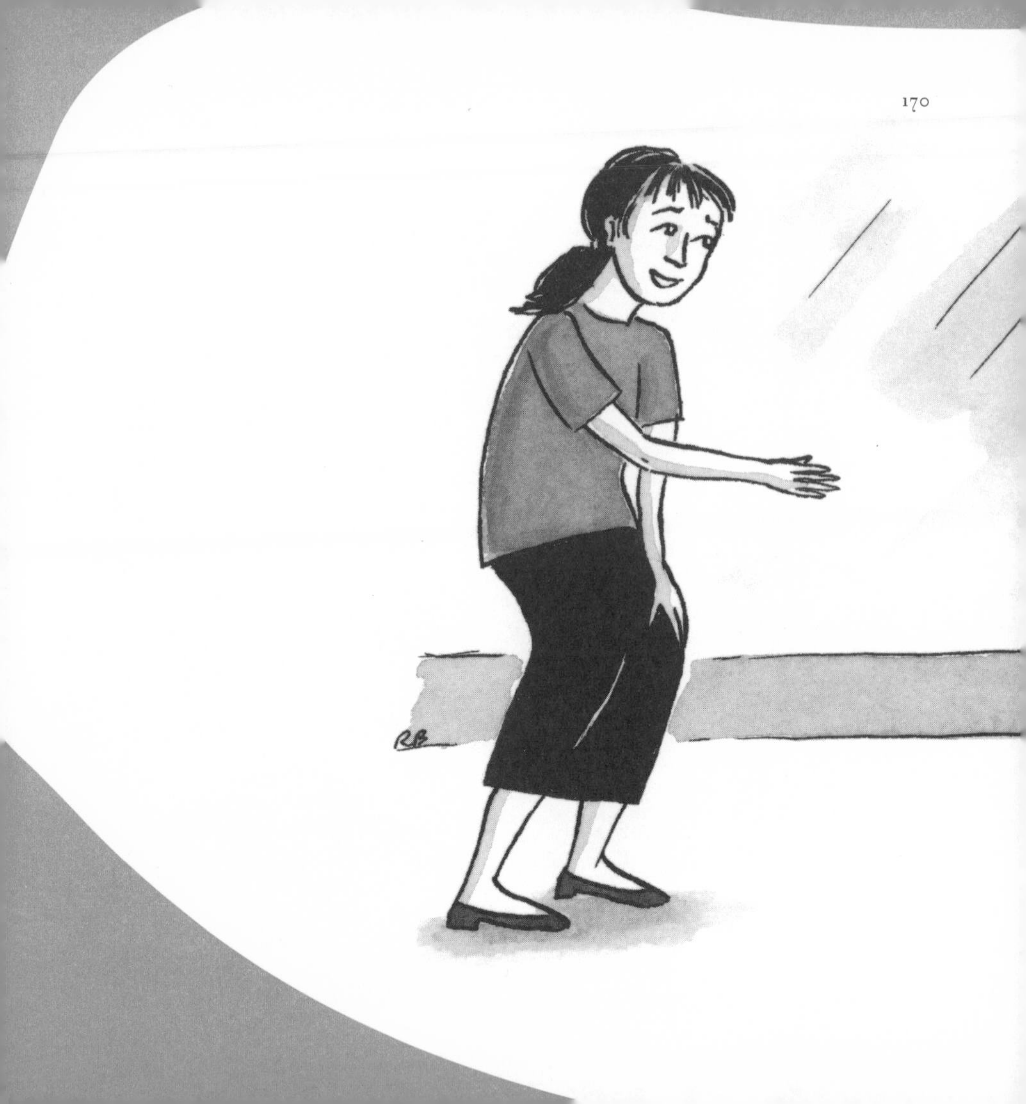
RB

If you think you shouldn't, don't.

No matter which line you pick in the grocery store, it will be the wrong one.

A woman with a lever, a ladder, and a compass can do anything a man can do.

Have a grand failed romance in your past.

The more strict you are with a teenage daughter, the more she will sneak out of the house to date a boy who works in an auto-body repair shop. It can't be helped.

If you can't beat them, at least
try to annoy them.

Never get involved with someone who has more problems than you do.

Having something to say
is overrated.

I wish I had known I didn't have to drag a man along on all my risk-taking adventures since I was the one supplying the courage.

Never get your heart set on a peanut butter and jelly sandwich until you're sure you have some jelly.

It's time to scrap the notion
that mothers are always kind, under-
standing, patient, and wise. Persistence
and grit should be given their due
weight as maternal virtues!

*There is no crisis in life that
cannot be faced better with
chocolate.*

Stop,

look,

and

listen.

Learn how to iron a shirt and thread a needle.

In this life you can be oh so smart,
or oh so pleasant. For years I was
smart. I recommend pleasant.

Patience is watching someone else sweep.

I wish I'd understood the difference between kind—a trait I still aspire to—and nice, which comes from the Latin stem meaning "ignorant" and "not knowing." I am in a recovery program for nice girls.

Humor is truth,
only faster.

Emulate Katharine
Hepburn and Spencer
Tracy as needed.

One size
never fits all.

Never ask a woman when her
baby is due.

People argue because
they're both right.

Contributors

Mary Anderson, Lynne Bosche, Eileen McCann, Barry Thorpe, Dan Henry, Marsh Rose, Mark Sloan, Rich LeBlond, Ray LeBlond, Gene Daly, Cassandra Dunn, Dean Backus, Harriet McNamara, Sherina Cadnum, Laiko Bahrs, Stephanie Lucas, Charlie Anderson, Rick Boyer, Terry Duke, Marisa Davis, David Cardenas, Dan Heist, Susan Piper Pryor, Irish Waters, Debbie Farson, Mike Sochacki, Marc Cardinalli, Susan G. Seitz, Steve Pantel, Denise Johnson, Teresa R. Brown, Donna Leaf, Liz Roberts, Jackie Winspear, Kirsten Armstrong, Kara Parsons, Cindy Smith, Cynthia Bocoboc, Brad Newsham, Linda Kilby, Adrian Isola, Cathy Brooks, Merre Jayne McFate, Shannon Varney, Mitch Ratcliffe, Annie Lamott, Ken Lamott, Enoch Deutsch, Linda Hunter, Bill LeBlond, Barbara Schneider, Diane Morgan, Teresa Crouch, Kathleen Roarty, Connie King, Gina Ruzzo, Linda Knestaut, Jean Hashagen, Mary Jo Bowling, Bill Coy, Shawn Greene, Robin Clements, Melissa Miller, Sarah MacDonald, David Cummings, Janice Crow, Antoinette Stihl, Alden Olmsted, Karen Majkut, Peter Dewees, Morgan Heig, Susan Seitz-West, Rob Pegoraro, David Bedno, Mike Ayer, Carole Lewis, Lynn Befera, Gary LaRochelle, Molly Bannister, Kenneth Caldwell, Richard Reiss, Robin Adams, Maureen McVerry, Ari Kahn, Victoria Werhan, Barry Freidman, Julie Knight, Peggy Vincent, Pat Milton, Leslie A. Gordon, Laura Jacoby, Samantha Pinney, Anne Milner, Joan Steinau Lester, Marilyn Penland, Nancy Brenner, Ginger Casey, Rodney Penland, Rosie Ruley, Bob Rudolph, Dee Dee Drake, George Devine, Richard Reiss, Sallie Shippen, Pam Engel, Susan Huch, Kristin Jerome, Karen Judge, Mary Ellen Lemieux, Sara Cakebread, Bill Johnson, Jim Broshar, Audrey Irvine-Broque.

If you have your own lessons from the *real* real world that you would like to share, please send them to Adair Lara at alara@sfchronicle.com; via her Web site www.adairlara.com; or c/o Chronicle Books LLC, 85 Second Street, San Francisco, CA 94105.